What Happens When I Sweat?

By Lincoln James

Gareth Stevens
Publishing

Please visit our website, www.garethstevens.com. For a free color catalog of all our high-quality books, call toll free 1-800-542-2595 or fax 1-877-542-2596.

Library of Congress Cataloging-in-Publication Data

James, Lincoln.
What happens when I sweat / by Lincoln James.
  p. cm — (My body does strange stuff)
Includes index.
ISBN 978-1-4339-9348-0 (pbk)
ISBN 978-1-4339-9349-7 (6-Pack)
ISBN 978-1-4339-9347-3 (library binding)
1. Perspiration — Juvenile literature. 2. Reflexes — Juvenile literature. I. James, Lincoln. II. Title
QP221.J26 2013
612.7921—dc23

Published in 2014 by
Gareth Stevens Publishing
111 East 14th Street, Suite 349
New York, NY 10003

Designer: Michael J. Flynn
Editor: Greg Roza

Photo credits: Cover, p. 1 © iStockphoto.com/nycshooter; p. 5 AISPIX by Image Source/Shutterstock.com; p. 7 Kzenon/Shutterstock.com; p. 9 Andrea Danti/ Shutterstock.com; p. 11 (main image) © iStockphoto.com/AnnaZ; p. 11 (inset) Scott Kleinman/Stone/Getty Images; p. 13 Thomas Barwick/Digital Vision/Getty Images; p. 15 Lisa F. Young/Shutterstock.com; p. 17 PhotoAlto/Laurence Mouton/PhotoAlto Agency RF Collections/Getty Images; p. 19 iStockphoto.com/studio9400; p. 20 344518471/Shutterstock.com.

Printed in the United States of America

CPSIA compliance information: Batch #CS13GS: For further information contact Gareth Stevens, New York, New York at 1-800-542-2595.

Contents

Boldface words appear in the glossary.

Getting Sweaty!

When you play a sport or ride your bike, you sweat. You might even sweat on a hot day without doing anything at all. Sweating might seem gross, but it's important. It's our body's way of cooling off.

Body Temperature

Your body likes to stay the same **temperature** all the time—98.6°F (37°C). When you're active or the day is hot, your body temperature can rise. This can also happen when you're sick. When your body temperature rises, you may start to sweat.

How We Sweat

When your body gets too hot, it sends messages to your brain. The brain sends messages to special **organs** called sweat glands. A gland is an organ that makes something the body needs to work properly. Sweat glands make sweat.

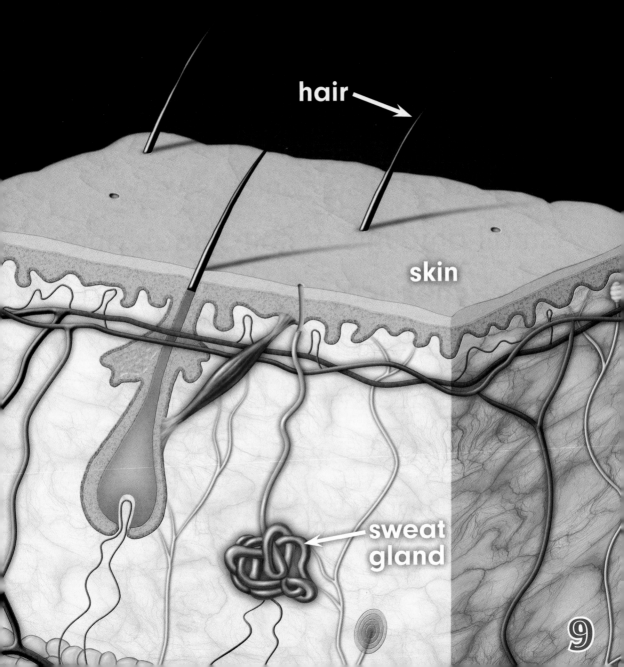

hair →

skin

sweat gland ←

9

Our sweat is made almost entirely of water. It also contains very small amounts of salt, sugar, and other **chemicals**. Sweat exits the skin though tiny holes called pores. Once sweat is outside the body, it's sometimes called perspiration (puhr-spuh-RAY-shun).

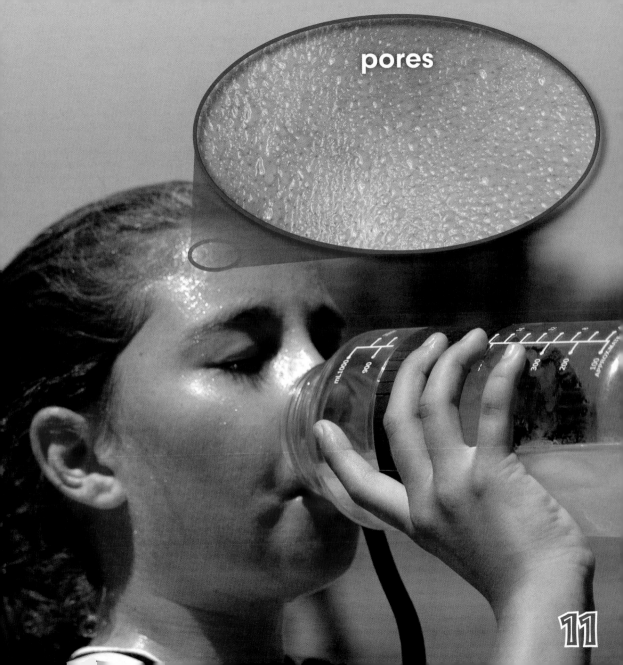

Why Do We Sweat?

Our body temperature rises when we're active. This can also happen on a hot day. Air makes sweat on your skin **evaporate**, which helps cool you off. This keeps your body temperature from getting too high, which can be dangerous.

13

Sometimes you may sweat when you're nervous or scared. During these times, glands in your body work harder to make chemicals that help you deal with these feelings. Some of these chemicals affect the sweat glands and make you sweat.

You may also sweat when you're sick or have a fever. However, sweating too much every day can mean something is wrong. Listen to your body. If you commonly sweat for no reason, you should go see a doctor.

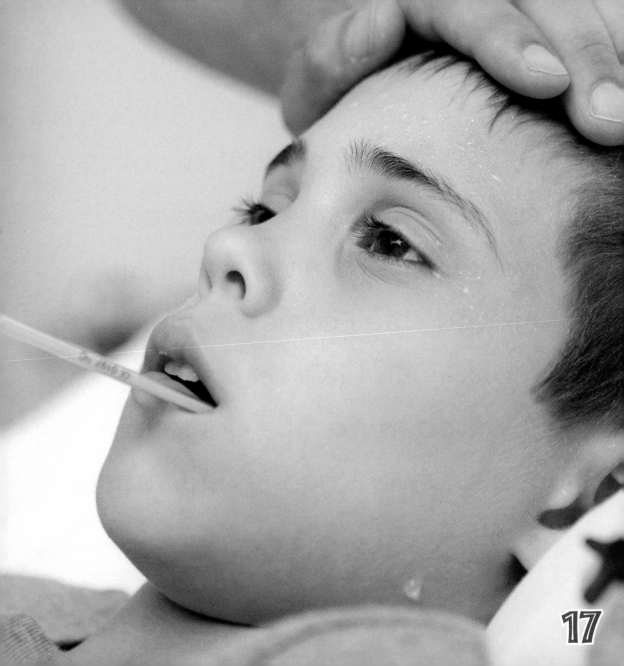

17

I Stink!

Most people know that sweat can make you stink. However, sweat itself has no smell at all. The bad smell comes from tiny creatures that live on our skin called **bacteria**. The bacteria feed on sweat and change it into chemicals that stink!

19

Replace Your Water

It's important to drink a lot of water when you're playing a sport because your body loses water when you sweat. If your body runs low on water, you may feel tired and achy. If you don't replace your body's water, you can even get very sick.

COOLING OFF

body temperature rises

↓

body sends messages to brain

↓

brain sends messages to sweat glands

↓

sweat glands make sweat

↓

sweat comes out of pores

↓

sweat evaporates and cools body

Glossary

bacteria: tiny creatures that can only be seen with a microscope

chemical: matter that can be mixed with other matter to cause changes

evaporate: to change from a liquid to a gas

organ: a body part

temperature: how hot or cold something is

For More Information

Books

Barnhill, Kelly Regan. *The Sweaty Book of Sweat.* Mankato, MN: Capstone Press, 2010.

Stewart, Melissa. *The Skin You're In: The Secrets of Skin.* New York, NY: Marshall Cavendish Benchmark, 2011.

Websites

KidsHealth
kidshealth.org/kid
Find more information about sweating and many other health topics.

What Is Skin?
health.howstuffworks.com/skin-care/beauty/sun-care/sunscreen1.htm
Check out this webpage to learn more about how skin works and what's inside it, including sweat glands.

Index